EASY GUITAR

THE
Eric Clapton
BOOK

T0050954

Cover Photo by Mick Hutson / RETNA, LTD.

This publication is not for sale in
the EU and/or Australia
or New Zealand.

ISBN 0-7935-8313-6

HAL•LEONARD®
CORPORATION
7777 W. BLUEMOUND RD. P.O. BOX 13819 MILWAUKEE, WI 53213

Visit Hal Leonard Online at
www.halleonard.com

EASY GUITAR

CONTENTS

4 Strum and Pick Patterns	26 Cocaine
	27 Comin' Home
5 After Midnight	34 Crossroads (Cross Road Blues)
6 Alberta	28 Evil (Is Going On)
7 All Your Love (I Miss Loving)	30 For Your Love
8 Anyone for Tennis	32 Forever Man
10 Baby What's Wrong	35 Further on Up the Road
12 Bad Love	36 Got to Get Better in a Little While
11 Badge	37 Got to Hurry
16 Before You Accuse Me (Take a Look at Yourself)	38 Hard Times
	42 Have You Ever Loved a Woman
14 Bell Bottom Blues	40 Heaven Is One Step Away
17 Bernard Jenkins	43 Hello Old Friend
20 Better Make It Through Today	46 Hey Hey
18 Blues Power	44 Hideaway
19 Boom Boom	47 Honey in Your Hips
22 Can't Find My Way Home	50 I Ain't Got You
23 A Certain Girl	48 I Can't Stand It
24 Change the World	51 I Feel Free

58 I Shot the Sheriff

54 I Wish You Would

56 I've Got a Rock 'n' Roll Heart

59 Key to the Highway

62 Knockin' on Heaven's Door

63 Lawdy Mama

60 Lay Down Sally

64 Layla

65 Layla (Acoustic Version)

66 Let It Grow

67 Let It Rain

68 Lonely Stranger

69 Malted Milk

70 Mean Old Frisco

71 Mean Old World

76 Miss You

72 Motherless Children

74 Nobody Knows You When You're Down and Out

77 Old Love

78 One More Chance

79 Only You Know and I Know

84 Presence of the Lord

80 Pretending

82 Promises

85 Ramblin' on My Mind

94 Roll It Over

86 Running on Faith

88 San Francisco Bay Blues

90 The Shape You're In

92 She's Waiting

95 Signe

98 Sleeping in the Ground

100 Someone Like You

102 Spoonful

105 Strange Brew

106 Sunshine of Your Love

108 Tales of Brave Ulysses

110 Tears in Heaven

112 Tell the Truth

114 Thorn Tree in the Garden

107 Too Bad

116 Tulsa Time

117 Walkin' Blues

118 Watch Out for Lucy

120 Whatcha Gonna Do

122 White Room

128 Willie and the Hand Jive

124 Wonderful Tonight

126 Wrapping Paper

STRUM AND PICK PATTERNS

This chart contains the suggested strum and pick patterns that are referred to by number at the beginning of each song in this book. The symbols ⊓ and ∨ in the strum patterns refer to down and up strokes, respectively. The letters in the pick patterns indicate which right-hand fingers plays which strings.

p = **thumb**
i = **index finger**
m = **middle finger**
a = **ring finger**

For example; Pick Pattern 2
is played: thumb - index - middle - ring

Strum Patterns   ## Pick Patterns

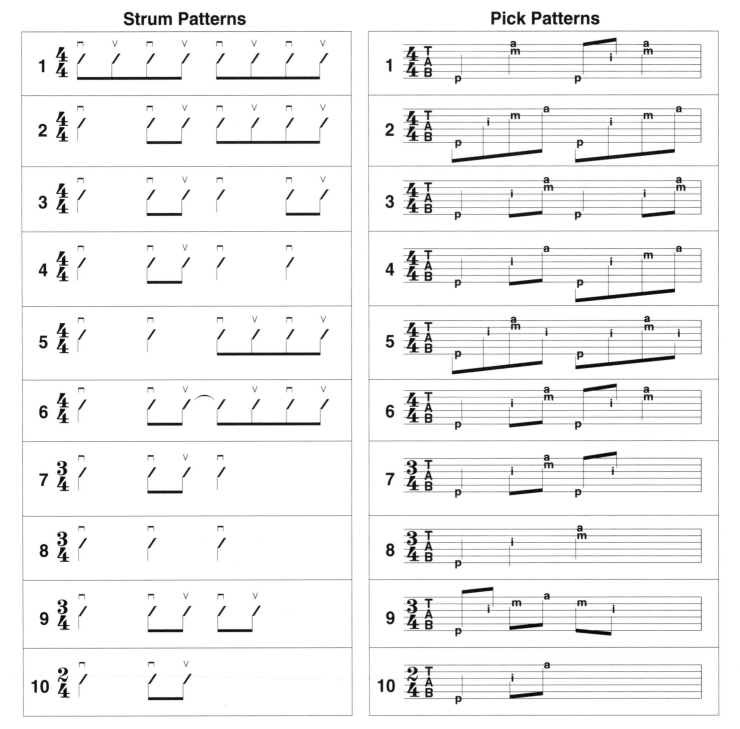

You can use the 3/4 Strum or Pick Patterns in songs written in compound meter (6/8, 9/8, 12/8, etc.).
For example, you can accompany a song in 6/8 by playing the 3/4 pattern twice in each measure.
The 4/4 Strum and Pick Patterns can be used for songs written in cut time (¢) by doubling the note time values in the patterns. Each pattern would therefore last two measures in cut time.

After Midnight

Words and Music by John J. Cale

Strum Pattern: 6
Pick Pattern: 5

Verse
Moderate Rock

1. Af - ter mid - night, __ we're gon - na let it all __ hang down. __
2. *See Additional Lyrics*

__ Af - ter mid - night, __ we're gon - na

chug - a - lug __ and shout. __ We're gon - na

stim - u - late __ some ac - tion; __ we're gon - na get some sat - is - fac - tion.

We're gon - na find out what it is all a - bout. __

Af - ter mid - night, __ we're gon - na let it all __ hang down. __

Outro

Af - ter mid - night, __ we're gon - na

Repeat and Fade

let it all __ hang down. __

Additional Lyrics

2. After midnight, we're gonna shake your tambourine,
After midnight, 's all gon' be peaches and cream.
Gonna cause talk and suspicion,
We're gonna give an exhibition,
We're gonna find out what it is all about.
After midnight, we gonna let it all hang down.

Alberta

New Words and New Music Adaptation by Huddie Ledbetter

Strum Pattern: 8
Pick Pattern: 8

Verse

Moderately

1. Al - ber - ta, Al - ber - ta, _____ where ya been so ___ long? __

2., 4., 5. *See Additional Lyrics*
3. *Instrumental*

Al - ber - ta, Al - ber - ta, ___

where ya been so long? __ Ain't had ___ no lov -

in' since you been _ gone. __ 2. Al - ber - ta, Al - ber -

since you've _ been ___ gone. ___

Additional Lyrics

2. Alberta, Alberta, where'd you stay last night?
   Alberta, Alberta, where'd you stay last night?
   Come home this mornin', clothes don't fit you right.

4. Alberta, Alberta, girl you're on my mind.
   Alberta, Alberta, girl you're on my mind.
   Ain't had no lovin' in such a great, long time.

5. Alberta, Alberta, where you been so long?
   Alberta, Alberta, where you been so long?
   Ain't had no lovin' since you've been gone.

All Your Love (I Miss Loving)

Words and Music by Otis Rush

Strum Pattern: 1
Pick Pattern: 2

Additional Lyrics

2. All your love, pretty baby, that I got in store for you.
   All your love, pretty baby, that I got in store for you.
   I love you pretty baby.
   Well, I say you love me too.

Chorus Hey, hey, baby.
   All your lovin', pretty baby,
   Hey, hey, baby.
   Yeah, yeah, yeah, yeah, yeah, baby,
   Oh, oh, baby.
   Just before I met you, baby,
   I never knew what I was missin'.

Anyone for Tennis

Words and Music by Eric Clapton and Martin Sharpe

Additional Lyrics

2. And the ice creams are all melting on the streets of bloody beer,
   While the beggars strain the pavements with flourescent Christmas cheer.
   And the Bentley driving guru is putting up his price.

Bridge The yellow Buddist monk is burning brightly at the zoo.
   You can bring a bowl of rice and then a glass of water too.
   And fate is setting up the chessboard while death rolls out the dice.

Baby What's Wrong

By Jimmy Reed

Strum Pattern: 3
Pick Pattern: 3

Badge

Words and Music by Eric Clapton and George Harrison

Strum Pattern: 4
Pick Pattern: 6

Intro
Moderately

Verse

1. Think-in' 'bout the times you drove __ in my car. __
2., 3. *See Additional Lyrics*

Think-in' that I might have drove __ you too far.

And I'm think-in' 'bout the love that you laid on my ta-

To Coda

-ble.

Yes, I told __

Chorus

__ you that the light goes up and down. __ Don't you no - tice how the wheel goes

round. And you bet - ter pick your-self up from the ground __ be - fore __ they bring the cur - tain down.

D.S. al Coda

Coda

Yes, be - fore __ they bring the cur - tain down. __

Additional Lyrics

2. I told you not to wander 'round in the dark.
   I told you 'bout the swans, that they live in the park.
   Then I told you 'bout our kid, now he's married to Mabel.

3. Talkin' 'bout a girl that looks quite like you.
   She didn't have the time to wait in the queue.
   She cried away her life since she fell off the cradle.

Bad Love

Words and Music by Eric Clapton and Mick Jones

Strum Pattern: 3
Pick Pattern: 3

Intro
Moderately

1. Oh, what a feel - ing I

2. See Additional Lyrics

get when I'm ___ with you, ___ you take my heart in - to

ev - ery - thing ___ you do. ___ And it makes me sad ___ for the

Additional Lyrics

2. And now I see that my life has been so blue,
With all the heartaches I had till I met you.
But I'm glad to say now that's all behind me,
With you here by my side.
And there's no more memories to remind me,
Your love will keep me alive.

Bell Bottom Blues

Words and Music by Eric Clapton

Strum Pattern: 4

Pick Pattern: 4

Verse

Slow Rock

C

1. Bell bot-tom blues, you made me cry.

2., 3. *See Additional Lyrics*

E/B Am C/G

I don't want to

F G F C G C

lose _ this feel - in'. If I could choose _

E/B Am C/G F G

a place _ to die, ___ it would be in ___ your _ arms.

Chorus

A E F#m

Do you wan-na see me crawl a-cross _ the floor ___ to you? _

D E A E

Do you wan-na hear me beg you to take me back? _

F#m D E A

___ I'd glad - ly do it be - cause I don't want to

Additional Lyrics

2. It's all wrong, but it's all right,
   The way that you treat me, baby.
   Once I was strong, but I lost the fight.
   You won't find a better loser.

3. Bell bottom blues, don't say goodbye.
   I'm sure we're gonna meet again.
   And if we do, don't ya be surprised
   If you find me with another lover.

Before You Accuse Me
(Take a Look at Yourself)

Words and Music by Eugene McDaniels

Strum Pattern: 1
Pick Pattern: 2

Additional Lyrics

2. I called your mama 'bout three or four nights ago.
I called your mama 'bout three or four nights ago.
Well, your mama said "Son don't call my daughter no more."

3. Before you 'cuse me, take a look at yourself.
Before you 'cuse me, take a look at yourself.
You say I'm spendin' my money on other women,
You takin' money from someone else.

4. Come on back home, baby, try my love one more time.
Come on back home, baby, try my love one more time.
You know if things don't go to suit you, I think I'll lose my mind.

5. Before you 'cuse me, take a look at yourself.
Before you 'cuse me, take a look at yourself.
You say I'm spendin' my money on other women,
You takin' money from someone else.

Bernard Jenkins

By Eric Clapton

Strum Pattern: 1
Pick Pattern: 2

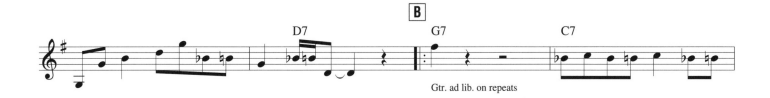

Blues Power

Words and Music by Eric Clapton and Leon Russell

Boom Boom

By John Lee Hooker

Strum Pattern: 3
Pick Pattern: 3

Moderate Shuffle

Verse

1. Boom, boom, boom, boom,
3. See Additional Lyrics

I'm gon - na shoot 'cha right down. Knock ya off your feet, take you home with me. ___ Put you in my house.

Boom, boom, boom, boom.

Verse

2. Boom, boom, boom, boom. ___
4. See Additional Lyrics

Yeah, yeah, yeah, yeah. ___ I ___ love to see you strut, when you're walk-in' to me. ___ When you're talk - in' to me, that knocks me out. ___

1.
Yeah, let's go! 3. Boom, boom,

2.
let's go!

Additional Lyrics

2. Boom, boom, boom, you know I like it like that.
   With your baby talk, oh and the way that you walk.
   You know it knocks me right down.
   Knocks me off my feet.

4. Boom, boom, boom, boom. Yeah, yeah, yeah, yeah.
   Oh, oh, oh, oh, now, now, now, now,
   Yeah, yeah, yeah, yeah, now, now, now, now.
   Let's go!

Better Make It Through Today

Words and Music by Eric Clapton

Strum Pattern: 4
Pick Pattern: 1

Verse
Slow Blues

1. "Life is what ___ you make it,"
3. *See Additional Lyrics*

that's what the peo - ple say, ___

and if I can't make it through ___ to - mor - row

I bet - ter make it through ___ to - day. ___

To Coda ⊕ **Verse**

2. "Life is what you

Additional Lyrics

3. I have had my share of troubles,
It's nothing new to me.
When I look around me
All I see is misery.

Can't Find My Way Home

Words and Music by Steve Winwood

A Certain Girl

Words and Music by Naomi Neville

Strum Pattern: 6
Pick Pattern: 5

Verse
Moderately Bright

1. Well, there's a cer - tain girl __ I've been in love with a long, long
2. *See Additional Lyrics*

time. __ (What's her name?) I can't tell ya. (No!) I can't re - veal __ her

name __ un - til I've got her. (What's her name?) I can't tell ya. (No!) Well, I've

Pre-Chorus

tried to get her time and time a - gain. We just a - end up as a -
See Additional Lyrics

Chorus

noth - ing but friends. There's a cer - tain girl __ I've been in love with a long, long

To Coda | **1.** time. __ (What's her name?) I can't tell ya. (No!) 2. Well, there's a | **2.** tell ya. (No!) Well, I've a *D.S. al Coda*

Coda

tell ya. (No!) I can't tell ya. (No.!) I can't tell ya. (No!) I can't tell ya.

Additional Lyrics

2. Well, there's a certain chick I've been sweet on since I met her.
   (What's her name?) I can't tell ya. (No!)
   I can't repeat her name until I get her.
   (What's her name?) I can't tell ya. (No!)

Pre-Chorus Well, one day I'm gonna wake up and say,
   "I'd do anything, just to be your slave."

Change the World

featured on the Motion Picture Soundtrack PHENOMENON

Words and Music by Gordon Kennedy, Tommy Sims and Wayne Kirkpatrick

Strum Pattern: 3
Pick Pattern: 4

Verse
Moderately

1. If I could reach the stars, ___ I'd pull one down for you, ___

shine it on my heart ___

so you could see the truth, ___ that this love in - side ___

is ev - 'ry - thing it seems. ___

But for now I find ___ it's on - ly in my dreams ___

Chorus

that I can change ___ the world. ___

Additional Lyrics

2. If I could be king
   Even for a day,
   I'd take you as my queen,
   I'd have it no other way.
   And our love would rule
   In this kingdom that we had made
   Till then I'll be a fool,
   Wishin' for the day...

Cocaine

Words and Music by John J. Cale

Strum Pattern: 1
Pick Pattern: 2

Intro
Moderate Rock

1. If you wan-na hang out, you've got-ta
2., 3. *See Additional Lyrics*

take her out; co-caine.

If you wan-na get down,

down on the ground; co-caine.

She don't lie,

Chorus

she don't lie, she don't lie; co-caine.

To Coda 1.

2.

D.S. al Coda

2. If you

3. If your

Coda

Outro-Chorus

Repeat and Fade

She don't lie, she don't lie, she don't lie; co-caine.

Additional Lyrics

2. If you got bad news,
   You wanna kick them blues, cocaine.
   When your day is done
   And ya wanna run, cocaine.

3. If your thing is gone.
   And ya wanna ride on, cocaine.
   Don't forget this fact,
   Can't get it back, cocaine.

Comin' Home

Words and Music by Eric Clapton and Bonnie Bramlett

Strum Pattern: 1
Pick Pattern: 2

Verse
Fast Rock

1. Been out __ on the road __ 'bout six months
2. *See Additional Lyrics*

too long. I want __ you so bad, __ I can __ hard-ly

stand it. I'm so __ tired, __ and I'm all a-lone. __

__ We'll soon __ be to-geth-er, __ and that's __ it.

1. I'm com-in' home __ to your __ love. __

Asus4 A   E A E

Asus4 A   2. to your love. __

Additional Lyrics

2. Hitchhikin' on the turnpike all day long.
Nobody seemed to notice; they just pass me over.
To keep from goin' crazy, I gotta sing my song.
Got a whole lot of lovin'.
And, baby, that's why I'm comin' home to your love.

Evil (Is Going on)

Words and Music by Willie Dixon

Strum Pattern: 3
Pick Pattern: 3

Additional Lyrics

2. You make it to your house,
   Knock on the front door.
   Run 'round to the back;
   You catch him just before he goes.

3. If you call on the telephone,
   And she answers long and slow.
   Grab the first thing smokin';
   An' you have-ta holler go home.

For Your Love

Words and Music by Graham Gouldman

Additional Lyrics

2. I'd give the moon if it were mine to give.
   For your love.
   I'd give the stars and the sun 'fore I live.

Forever Man

Words and Music by Jerry Lynn Williams

Strum Pattern: 3
Pick Pattern: 4

Verse
Moderate Rock

1. How man - y times ___ must I tell you, ba - by,
3. *Instrumental*

how man - y bridg - es I've got to cross? ___

How man - y times must I ex - plain my - self

'fore I can talk to the boss, ___

'fore I can talk to the boss? ___

Verse

2., 4. How man - y times ___ must I say I love ___ you ___

Crossroads (Cross Road Blues)

Words and Music by Robert Johnson

Strum Pattern: 1
Pick Pattern: 2

Additional Lyrics

2. I went down to the crossroad, tried to flag a ride.
   Down to the crossroad, tried to flag a ride.
   Nobody seemed to know me. Ev'rybody passed me by.

3. When I'm goin' down to Rosedale, take my rider by my side.
   Goin' down to Rosedale, take my rider by my side.
   We can still barrelhouse, baby, on the riverside.

4. You can run, you can run. Tell my friend, boy, Willie Brown.
   Run, you can run. Tell my friend, boy, Willie Brown.
   And I'm standin' at the crossroad. Believe I'm sinkin' down.

Further on Up the Road

Words and Music by Joe Veasey and Don Robey

Strum Pattern: 3
Pick Pattern: 3

Verse
Moderate Shuffle

1., 3. Fur-ther on up the road some-one's gon-na hurt you like you hurt me.
2. *See Additional Lyrics*

Fur-ther on up the road _ some-one's gon-na hurt you like you hurt me.

Fur-ther on up the road, ba - by, you just wait and see.

play 3 times

Outro

You been laugh-in' pret-ty ba - by; Some - day you're gon-na be cry - in'.

You been laugh-in' pret-ty ba - by; Some - day you're gon-na be cry - in'.

Fur-ther on up the road you'll find out I was-n't ly - in'.

Additional Lyrics

2. You got to reap just what you sow,
   That old saying is true.
   You got to reap just what you sow,
   That old saying is true.
   Just like you mistreat someone,
   Someone's gonna mistreat you.

Got to Get Better in a Little While

Words and Music by Eric Clapton

A   G   E   D   F#   F

Strum Pattern: 1
Pick Pattern: 2

Verse
Moderately Fast

A ... *G* ... *E*

1. Don't you know __ what's wrong with me? __ I'm
2., 3. *See Additional Lyrics*

A ... *G* ... *E* ... *A*

see-in' things I don't want to see. __ Sip-pin' things __ that ain't

G ... *E* ... *A*

good for me. __ I'm go-in' down fast, won't ya

Interlude

G ... *E* ... *D* ... *A* ... *E*

say a prayer __ for me. __

D ... *A* ... *E* ... *G*

Sun's got to shine _____

F# ... *F* ... *E* ... **6** ... |1. ... |2., 3. *2nd time, D.C. and Fade*

on my gui-tar __ some-day.

3. There's

Additional Lyrics

2. Revolution all across the land.
   Just like Sly you've got to make a stand.
   Please don't hurt nobody, don't knock 'em down.
   Give 'em a helping hand, to get up off the ground.

3. There's still one thing that you can do,
   Fall down on your knees and pray.
   I know the Lord's gonna answer you;
   Don't do it tomorrow, do it today.

Got to Hurry

By Oscar Rasputin

Strum Pattern: 1
Pick Pattern: 2

Hard Times

Words and Music by Ray Charles

Strum Pattern: 8
Pick Pattern: 8

Slow Blues

1. My moth-er told me

2. - 5. *See Additional Lyrics*
3. *Instrumental*

'fore she

passed a - way, ___ said, "Son, when I'm gone, ___ don't for -

get to pray ___ 'cause there'll be hard ___ times, ___ Lord, those

To Coda

hard ___ times." ___ Who knows ___ bet ter than ___

1., 2.

3.

___ I? ___

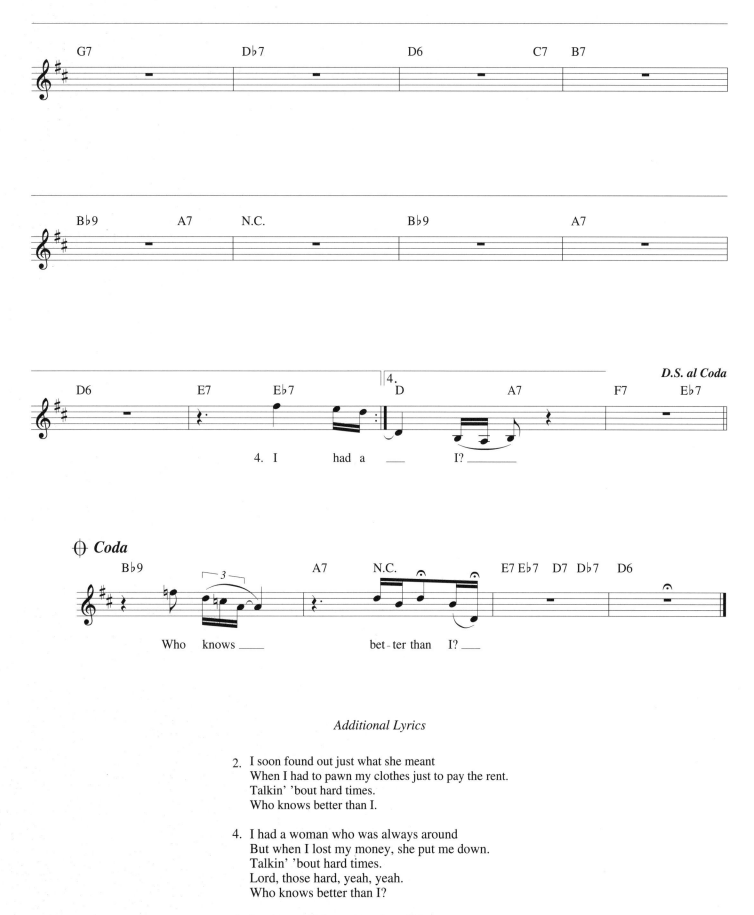

Additional Lyrics

2. I soon found out just what she meant
   When I had to pawn my clothes just to pay the rent.
   Talkin' 'bout hard times.
   Who knows better than I.

4. I had a woman who was always around
   But when I lost my money, she put me down.
   Talkin' 'bout hard times.
   Lord, those hard, yeah, yeah.
   Who knows better than I?

5. Lord, one of those days there'll be no more sorrow,
   But when I pass away.
   And no more hard times.
   No more hard, yeah, yeah.
   Who knows better than I?

Heaven Is One Step Away

Words and Music by Eric Clapton

Strum Pattern: 1
Pick Pattern: 2

Intro
Moderate Reggae

1., 3. We searched all through the night. _
2. And then there came the dawn: _

I could-n't find _ it;

you could-n't find _ it.

I knew _ some-thing was - n't right. _
I just _ had to car - ry on. _

I could-n't find _ it;

you could-n't find _ it, and they say heav - en is

Chorus

one step a - way. _

Heav - en is

Have You Ever Loved a Woman

Words and Music by Billy Myles

Strum Pattern: 8
Pick Pattern: 8

Verse
Moderate Blues

1. Have you ev-er loved _ a wom-an
2., 3. *See Additional Lyrics*

so _ much you trem-ble in pain? _

Have you ev-er loved _ a wom-an

so much you trem-ble in pain?

And all the

time, you know _____ she

bears _____ an-oth-er man's name. _____

1., 2.   3.

Additional Lyrics

2. But you just love that woman so much, it's a shame and a sin.
   You just love that woman so much, it's a shame and a sin.
   But all the time, you know she belongs to your very best friend.

3. Have you ever loved a woman, oh, you know you can't leave her alone?
   Have you ever loved a woman, yes, you know you can't leave her alone?
   Something deep inside of you won't let you wreck your best friend's home.

Hello Old Friend

Words and Music by Eric Clapton

Strum Pattern: 1
Pick Pattern: 2

Verse
Moderately Fast

1. As I was stroll - ing down __ the gar - den path, __
2., 3. *See Additional Lyrics*

I saw a flow - er glow - ing in __ the dark. __

It looked so pret - ty and __ it was u - nique __

I had to bend __ down just to have __ a peek. __ Hel - lo __ old friend, __

Chorus

__ (Hel - lo __ old friend. __) it's real - ly good __ to see __ you once a - gain. __

Hel - lo old friend, __ it's real - ly good __ to see __ you once a - gain. __
(Hel - lo __ old friend. __)

To Coda

2. I Hel - lo old friend; __

D.S. al Coda

Coda

Additional Lyrics

2. I saw you walking underneath the stars;
   I couldn't stop 'cause I was in a car.
   I'm sure the distance wouldn't be too far
   If I got out and walked to where you are.

3. An old man passed me by on the street today;
   I thought I knew him, but I couldn't say.
   I stopped to think if I could place his frame,
   But when he tipped his hat I knew his name.

Hideaway

By Freddy King and Sonny Thompson

C **Rock Beat**

2nd time, D.S. al Coda

⊕ *Coda*

Hey Hey

Words and Music by William "Big Bill" Broonzy

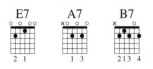

Strum Pattern: 4
Pick Pattern: 5

Moderately Fast

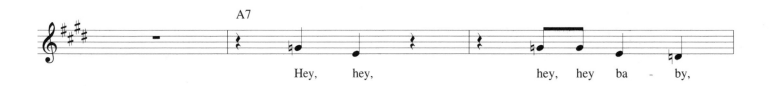

Honey in Your Hips

Words and Music by Keith Relf

Strum Pattern: 1
Pick Pattern: 2

Verse
Moderately

1. When I get out on the danc-ing floor, _____
2., 3. *See Additional Lyrics*

there ain't no stop-pin' me for an hour or more. _

I go rock-in' up and down and a-round and 'round. _____

I go reel-ing to the beat of that cra-zy sound. _   I

can't stop, I wan-na kiss your pret-ty lips, _   'cause I know, pret-ty babe, you got

1., 2.   *3.*

hon-ey in your hips. _   2. I

Additional Lyrics

2. I can't stop my feet and I can't stop my hands
   When I hear the sound of a rock 'n' roll band.
   Gotta rock, gotta roll, gotta jump and shout.
   Nobody better come and turn me out,
   I'm staying all night 'til I get my kicks,
   'Cause you know, pretty babe, you got honey in your hips.

3. I want you and-a you want me.
   We're gonna dance all night 'til we both feel free.
   We'll shake and we'll shimmy across the floor.
   When it gets late, we'll dance out the door.
   You better get ready with your pretty lips,
   'Cause you know, pretty babe, you got honey in your hips.

I Can't Stand It

Words and Music by Eric Clapton

Strum Pattern: 6
Pick Pattern: 5

Moderate Rock — **Verse**

Dm — Am

1. You've been told, _____ so may-be it's time ___ that you learned.
2., 3. *See Additional Lyrics*

G — Dm

You've been sold, _____

Am — G — *To Coda*

may-be it's time ___ that you earned. ___ I can't stand _

Chorus

Am — F — G — Am

___ it. You're fool-in' a-round. ___ I {can't / won't} stand ___ it. You're

F — G — Am — F — G

run-ning a-round. _ I {won't / can't} stand ___ it. Fool-in' a-round _ with my heart. _

Additional Lyrics

2. I'll explain, I feel like I'm bein' used.
   Make it plain, so you don't get confused.

3. It was time, time for me to let you know.
   Ain't no crime, no crime to let your feelings show.

I Ain't Got You

By Calvin Carter

Strum Pattern: 1
Pick Pattern: 2

Verse

Moderately Bright Shuffle

1. I got a Mas-er-at-i G. E. T. with a
2., 3., 4. *See Additional Lyrics*

snake-skin up-hol-ster-y. I got a charge ac-count at Gold-blatt's but I

ain't got you. 2. Got a Got a tav-ern ___ and a

li-quor store; I play the num-bers, yeah, four, for-ty-four. I got a

mo-jo, yeah, don't you know? ___ I'm all dressed up with no

place to go. 3., 4. I've got No, I ain't got you. I've got a

No, I ain't got you. No, I ain't got you. ___

Additional Lyrics

2. Got a closet full of clothes, but no matter where it goes,
   You keep the ring in my nose, but I ain't got you.

3., 4. I've got women to the right of me, I've got women to the left of me.
   I've got women all around me, but I ain't got you.

I Feel Free

Words and Music by Jack Bruce and Pete Brown

E7#9   B   D   E   C   Bb   A   F

Strum Pattern: 3
Pick Pattern: 3

Intro
Fast Rock

E7#9   N.C.

Bum, bum, bum, ba, bum, ___ bum.   Bum, bum, bum, ba, bum, ___

___ bum. I ___ feel free. Bum, bum, bum, ba, bum, ___ bum. I ___ feel free. Hmm, ___

___ hmm, hmm, hmm, hmm, hmm, hmm. ___ **1.** Hmm, ___ hmm, hmm, hmm,

2. hmm. Hmm, ___ hmm _ hmm, hmm, hmm.   B D E

Chorus

E   D   E   D   E

Feel ___ when ___ I dance with you.   We ___
See Additional Lyrics

D   E   D   E   D

___ move like the sea.   You, ___ you're all I

E   D   E

want to know.   I ___ feel ___ free.

Additional Lyrics

Chorus Dance floor is like the sea.
Ceiling is the sky.
You're the sun, and as you shine on me,
I feel free.
I feel free.
I feel free.

I Wish You Would

Words and Music by Billy Boy Arnold

Strum Pattern: 3
Pick Pattern: 3

Intro
Fast Rock

Ear - ly in the morn - in', 'bout the break of day,

that's when my ba - by went a - way.

Come back, ba - by, I wish you would. 'Cause

To Coda

cry - in' and a - plead - in' won't do no good.

Verse

Hug - gin' and a - kiss - in' and a late at night,

tell ya now, ba - by, I feel just right.

I've Got a Rock 'n' Roll Heart

Words and Music by Troy Seals, Eddie Setser and Steve Diamond

Additional Lyrics

2. Feels like we're falling into the arms of the night,
So if you're not ready, don't be holding me so tight.
I guess there's nothing left for me to explain.
Here's what you're getting, and I don't wanna change, I don't wanna change.

I Shot the Sheriff

Words and Music by Bob Marley

Strum Pattern: 3
Pick Pattern: 3

Additional Lyrics

2. Sheriff John Brown always hated me;
   For what, I don't know.
   And every time that I plant a seed,
   He said, "Kill it before it grows,"
   "Kill it before it grows."

3. Freedom came my way one day,
   So I started out of town.
   All of a sudden, I see Sheriff Brown
   Aimin' to shoot me down,
   So I shot him down.

4. Reflexes got the better of me,
   What will be will be.
   Everyday, the bucket goes to the well,
   One day the bottom will drop out
   I say, one day the bottom will drop out.

Key to the Highway

Words and Music by Big Bill Broonzy and Chas. Segar

Lay Down Sally

Words and Music by Eric Clapton, Marcy Levy and George Terry

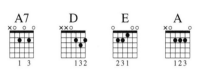

Strum Pattern: 1
Pick Pattern: 2

Additional Lyrics

2. The sun ain't nearly on the rise,
   And we still got the moon and stars above.
   Underneath the velvet skies, love is all that matters.
   Won't you stay with me?
   And don't you ever leave.

3. I long to see the morning light
   Coloring your face so dreamily.
   So don't you go and say goodbye,
   You can lay your worries down and stay with me.
   And don't you ever leave.

Knockin' on Heaven's Door

Music and Lyrics by Bob Dylan

Strum Pattern: 4
Pick Pattern: 1

Verse
Moderately

1., 3. Ma,   take this badge   off of   me.
2. *See Additional Lyrics*
4. *Instrumental*

I can't use it an-y-more. ___

It's get-ting dark, too dark

to see.

I feel like I'm knock-in' on heav-en's door.

Chorus

Knock, knock knock-in' on heav-en's door.

Knock, knock knock-in' on heav-en's

door.

Knock, knock knock-in' on heav-en's door.

1., 2., 3.

Knock, knock knock-in' on heav-en's door.

4.   *D.C. and Fade*

door.

Additional Lyrics

2. Ma, take these guns away from me.
I can't shoot them any more.
There's a long black cloud following me.
I feel like I'm knockin' on heaven's door.

Lawdy Mama

Traditional

Arranged by Eric Clapton

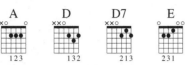

Strum Pattern: 3
Pick Pattern: 3

Layla

Words and Music by Eric Clapton and Jim Gordon

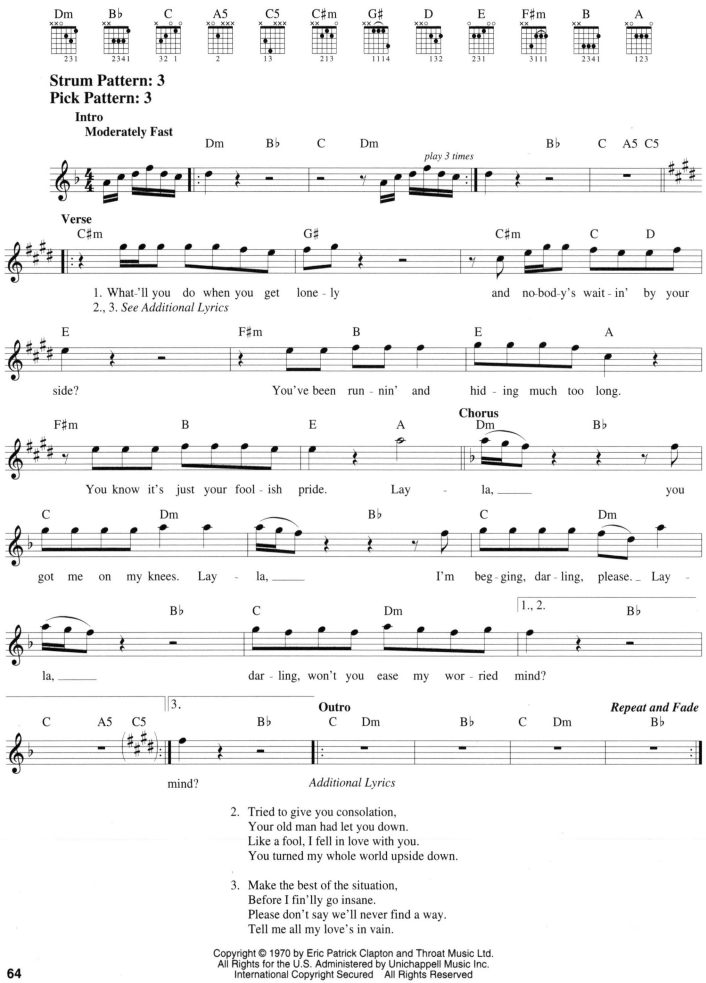

Strum Pattern: 3
Pick Pattern: 3

Intro
Moderately Fast

Verse

1. What'll you do when you get lone - ly and no-bod-y's wait - in' by your
2., 3. *See Additional Lyrics*

side? You've been run - nin' and hid - ing much too long.

You know it's just your fool - ish pride. Lay - la, _____ you

got me on my knees. Lay - la, _____ I'm beg - ging, dar - ling, please. _ Lay -

la, _____ dar - ling, won't you ease my wor - ried mind?

mind?

Additional Lyrics

2. Tried to give you consolation,
Your old man had let you down.
Like a fool, I fell in love with you.
You turned my whole world upside down.

3. Make the best of the situation,
Before I fin'lly go insane.
Please don't say we'll never find a way.
Tell me all my love's in vain.

Layla (Acoustic Version)

Words and Music by Eric Clapton and Jim Gordon

Strum Pattern: 3
Pick Pattern: 3

Additional Lyrics

2. Tried to give you consolation,
   Your old man had let you down.
   Like a fool, I fell in love with you.
   You turned my whole world upside down.

3. Make the best of the situation,
   Before I finally go insane.
   Please don't say we'll never find a way.
   Tell me all my love's in vain.

Let It Grow

Words and Music by Eric Clapton

Strum Pattern: 1
Pick Pattern: 2

Verse
Moderately

1. Stand-ing at the cross - roads try'n to read the signs to tell me which way I should
2., 3. *See Additional Lyrics*

go to find the an - swer and all the time I know. Plant your love and let it

Chorus

grow. Let it grow, let it grow.

Let it blos - som, let it flow. In the sun, the rain, the

snow. Love is love - ly, let it

grow. let it let it grow, let it

Outro
Repeat and Fade

grow.

Additional Lyrics

2. Looking for a reason to check out on my mind.
   Trying hard to get a friend that I can count on,
   But there's nothing left to show.
   Plant your love and let it grow.

3. Time is getting shorter, there's much for you to do.
   Only ask and you will get what you are needing,
   The rest is up to you.
   Plant your love and let it grow.

Let It Rain

Words and Music by Eric Clapton and Bonnie Bramlett

Strum Pattern: 2
Pick Pattern: 4

Additional Lyrics

2. My life was like a desert flower,
Burning in the sun.
Until I found the way to love,
This heart was sad and done.

3. Now I know the secret;
There is nothing that I lack.
If I give my love to you,
Be sure to give it back.

Lonely Stranger

Words and Music by Eric Clapton

Strum Pattern: 3
Pick Pattern: 3

Verse

Moderately Slow Rock

1. I must be ___ in-vis-i-ble. ___ No one ___ knows ___ me. ___
2., 3., 4. *See Additional Lyrics*

___ I have crawled ___ down dead-end streets ___ on my hands and knees. ___

1., 3. *2., 4.*

'Cause

Chorus

I'm ___ a lone-ly stran-ger here ___ well be-yond ___ my day,

but I don't know what's go-in' on, ___ so I'll be on my way.

Yes, I will. Yes, I will. Yes, I

1. *D.C.* *2.*

will. will. Yes, I will.

Additional Lyrics

2. I was born with a raging thirst,
   A hunger to be free.
   But I've learned through the years,
   Don't encourage me.

3. When I walk, stay behind,
   Don't get close to me.
   'Cause it's sure to end in tears,
   So just let me be.

4. Some will say that I'm no good,
   Maybe I agree.
   Take a look, then walk away,
   That's alright with me.

Malted Milk

Words and Music by Robert Johnson

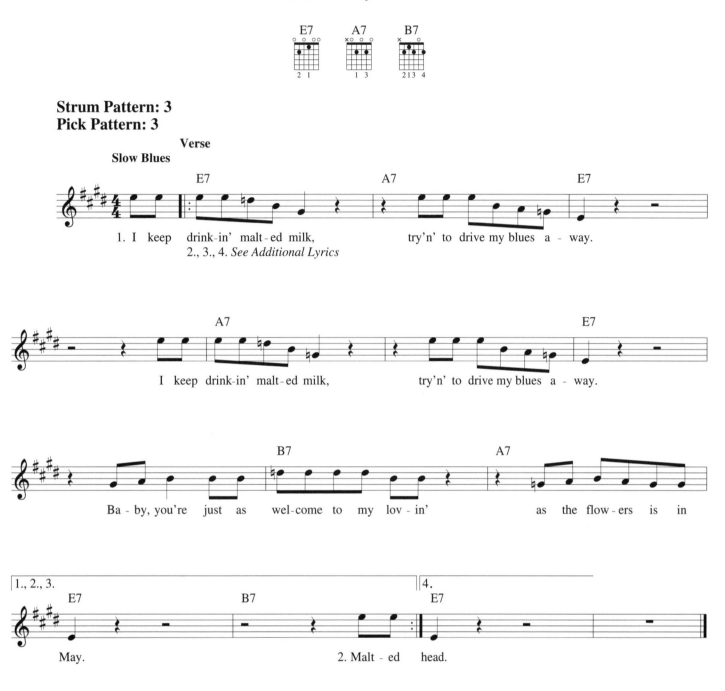

Strum Pattern: 3
Pick Pattern: 3

Additional Lyrics

2. Malted milk, malted milk, keep rushin' to my head.
   Malted milk, malted milk, keep rushin' to my head.
   And I have a funny, funny feelin', and I'm talkin' all out my head.

3. Baby, fix me one more drink 'n' hug your daddy one more time.
   Baby, fix me one more drink 'n' hug your daddy one more time.
   Keep on stirrin' my malted milk, mama, until I change my mind.

4. My doorknob keeps on turnin', there must be spooks around my bed.
   My doorknob keeps on turnin', there must be spooks around my bed.
   An' I have a funny, funny feelin', and the hair is risin' on my head.

Mean Old Frisco

Words and Music by Arthur Crudup

Strum Pattern: 3
Pick Pattern: 3

Additional Lyrics

2. Well, my mama, she done told me and my papa told me too,
   Mama told me, and my papa told me too.
   Woman get in your face, son, she ain't no friend to you.

3. Well, I'm goin' 'way now, baby, and your cryin' won't make me stay.
   Goin' 'way, baby, and your cryin' won't make me stay.
   Well, the more you cry, little girl, drive me away.

Mean Old World

By Walter Jacobs

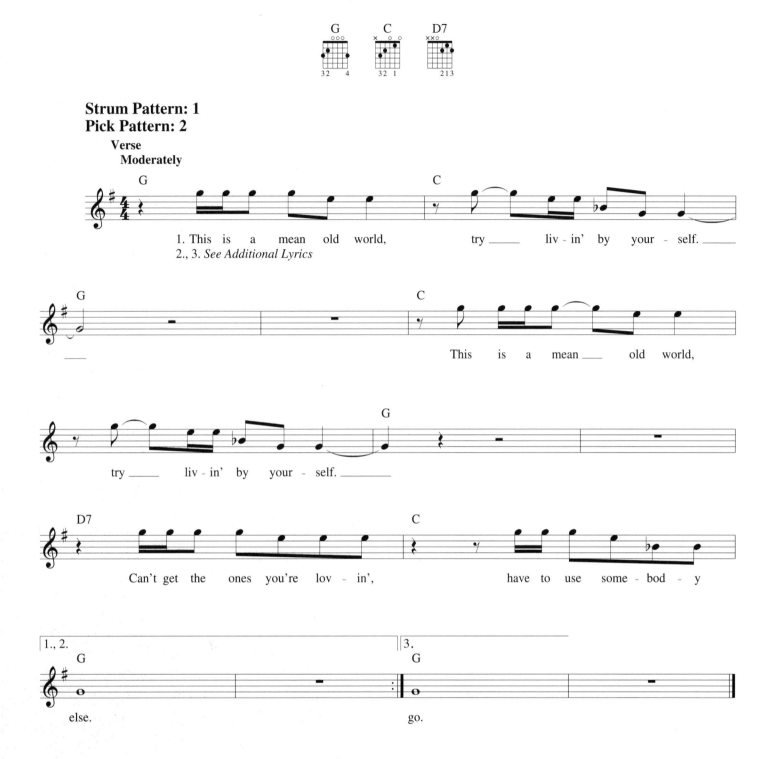

Strum Pattern: 1
Pick Pattern: 2

Verse
Moderately

1. This is a mean old world, try _____ liv-in' by your-self. _____
2., 3. *See Additional Lyrics*

This is a mean _____ old world,

try _____ liv-in' by your-self. _____

Can't get the ones you're lov-in', have to use some-bod-y

1., 2.

else.

3.

go.

Additional Lyrics

2. I've got the blues, I'll pack my things and go.
   I've got the blues, I'll pack my things and go.
   I guess you don't love me, lucky Mister So and So.

3. Sometimes I wonder why can your love be so cold;
   Sometimes I wonder why can your love be so cold.
   Guess you don't love me, gonna pack my things and go.

Motherless Children

Arranged by Eric Clapton and Carl Radle

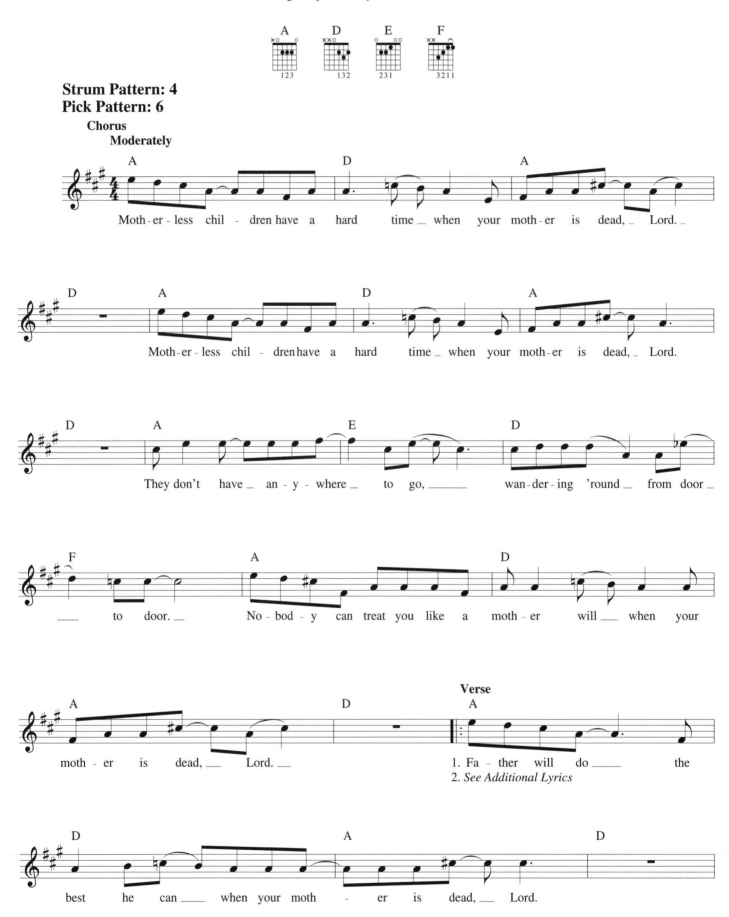

Strum Pattern: 4
Pick Pattern: 6

Chorus
Moderately

Moth-er-less chil - dren have a hard time _ when your moth-er is dead, _ Lord. _

Moth-er-less chil - dren have a hard time _ when your moth-er is dead, _ Lord.

They don't have _ an-y-where _ to go, _____ wan-der-ing 'round _ from door _

_____ to door. _ No-bod-y can treat you like a moth-er will _ when your

moth-er is dead, _ Lord. _

Verse

1. Fa-ther will do _____ the
2. *See Additional Lyrics*

best he can _____ when your moth - er is dead, _ Lord.

Additional Lyrics

2. Sister will do the best she can when your mother is dead, Lord.
   Sister will do the best she can when your mother is dead, Lord.
   Sister will do the best she can so many things a sister can't understand.
   Nobody treats you like a mother will when your mother is dead.

Nobody Knows You When You're Down and Out

Words and Music by Jimmie Cox

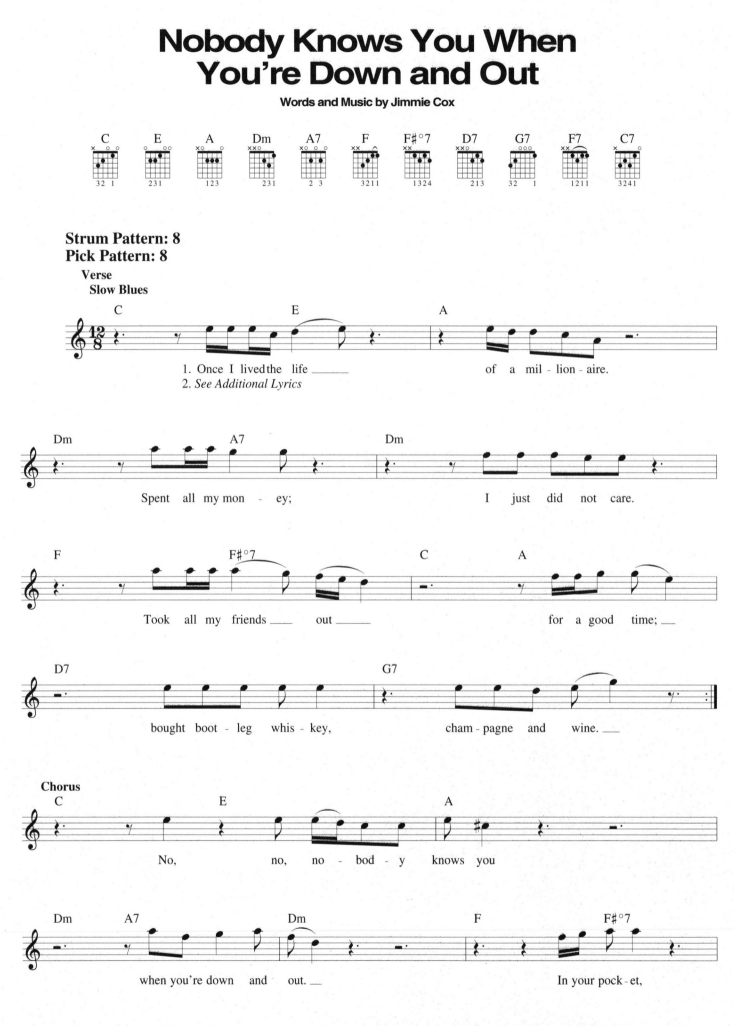

MCA music publishing

Additional Lyrics

2. Then I began to fall so low.
   Lost all my good friends; I didn't have nowhere to go.
   I get my hands on a dollar again,
   I'm gonna hang on to it till the eagle grins, yeah.

Miss You

Words and Music by Eric Clapton, Bobby Columby and Gregory Phillinganes

Strum Pattern: 3
Pick Pattern: 3

Additional Lyrics

2. No, don't say a word.
   I already heard that you don't love me.
   In your state of mind
   I don't need to hear your side of the story.

Pre-Chorus 2. Your friends all said that we had a future,
   But I don't think I really want to know,
   But friends keep telling me to lose you,
   And how glad they'll be when you decide to go.

Pre-Chorus 3. I broke my back to make you happy.
   Sometime, somehow, someone's got to pay.
   If you think you're better off without me,
   Just remember, it's a dirty world out there.

Old Love

Words and Music by Eric Clapton and Robert Cray

Strum Pattern: 3
Pick Pattern: 3

Verse
Moderately

1. I can feel _____ your bod-y when I'm ly-ing in my bed. _____
2. *See Additional Lyrics*
3. *Instrumental*

Too much _ con-fu - sion go-in' round through my_

_ head. _____ Makes me so _ an-gry to know that the flame still burns.

Why can't I get o - ver? _____ When will I ev-er learn? _

Chorus

Old love _____ leave me a-lone.

To Coda

Old love _____ go on home. _

1.

2. *D.C. al Coda*

Coda

Outro

Repeat and Fade

Additional Lyrics

2. I can see your face, but I know that it's not real,
   Just an illusion caused by how I used to feel.
   Makes me so angry to know that the flame still burns.
   Why can't I get over? When will I ever learn?
   Old love leave me alone.
   Old love go on home.

One More Chance

Words and Music by Eric Clapton

Strum Pattern: 3
Pick Pattern: 3

Additional Lyrics

2. Well, the sun won't shine and it refused to rain.
   And I banged my head, but I feel no pain.
   When I tell myself that I can start anew,
   But I know darn well it all depends on you.

3. So if you hear me say don't change your mind
   And give a thought to me, I won't be hard to find.
   And I promise you I'll do the best I can.
   Change my evil ways, and be your lovin' man.

Only You Know and I Know

Words and Music by Dave Mason

Strum Pattern: 3
Pick Pattern: 3

Additional Lyrics

2. I don't mean to mislead you.
   It's just my craziness coming through.
   But when it comes down to just two,
   I ain't no crazier than you.

3. We're both here to be pleasin',
   Oh, no, no, not deceivin'.
   But it's hard to believe in
   When you've been so mistreated.

Pretending

Words and Music by Jerry Williams

Strum Pattern: 3
Pick Pattern: 3

Additional Lyrics

3. Satisfied but lost in love, situations change.
   You're never who you used to think you are, how strange.

4. I get lost in alibis, sadness can't prevail.
   Everybody knows strong love can't fail.

Promises

Words and Music by Richard Feldman and Roger Linn

Strum Pattern: 3
Pick Pattern: 3

Verse
Country Rock

1. I don't care __ if you nev - er come home. I don't mind __ if you just __
2. See Additional Lyrics

__ keep on row - in' a - way __ on a dis - tant sea __ 'cause I don't __

__ love you __ and you don't __ love me. 2. You

Bridge

La, la, la, la, la, __ la, __ la.

La, la, la, la, la, __ la, __ la.

Verse

3. I don't care __ what you do __
4. See Additional Lyrics

Additional Lyrics

2. You cause a commotion when you come to town.
   You give 'em a smile and they melt.
   Havin' lovers and friends is all good and fine.
   But I don't like yours and you don't like mine.

4. I tried to love you for years upon years.
   You refused to take me for real.
   It's time you saw what I want you to see
   And I'd still love you if you'd just love me.

Presence of the Lord

Words and Music by Eric Clapton

Strum Pattern: 3
Pick Pattern: 3

Verse
Slowly

1., 3. I have fi - n'ly found a way to live ____ just like I nev-er could be-fore. ____

2. *See Additional Lyrics*

I know that I don't have much to give, ____

but I can o - pen an - y door. ____ Ev - 'ry-bod - y knows the se -

- cret, ev - 'ry-bod - y knows the score. ____

To Coda

I have fi - n'ly found a way to live ____ in the col - our of ____ the Lord. ____

D.C. al Coda

In the pres - ence of the Lord.

Coda

In the col - our of ____ the Lord. ____

Additional Lyrics

2. I have fin'ly found a place to live
Just like I never could before,
And I know I don't have much to give.
But soon I'll open any door.
Ev'rybody knows the secret,
Ev'rybody knows the score.
I have fin'ly found a place to live
In the presence of the Lord.

Ramblin' on My Mind

Words and Music by Robert Johnson

Strum Pattern: 1
Pick Pattern: 2

Additional Lyrics

2. I'm goin' down to the station, catch that old fast milk train, you'll see.
   I'm goin' down to the station, catch that old fast milk train, you'll see.
   I've got the blues 'bout Miss So and So, and the sun got the blues 'bout me.

3. I got mean things, I've got mean things all on my mind.
   Little girl, little girl, I've got mean things all on my mind.
   Is to leave my baby, 'cause she treat me so unkind.

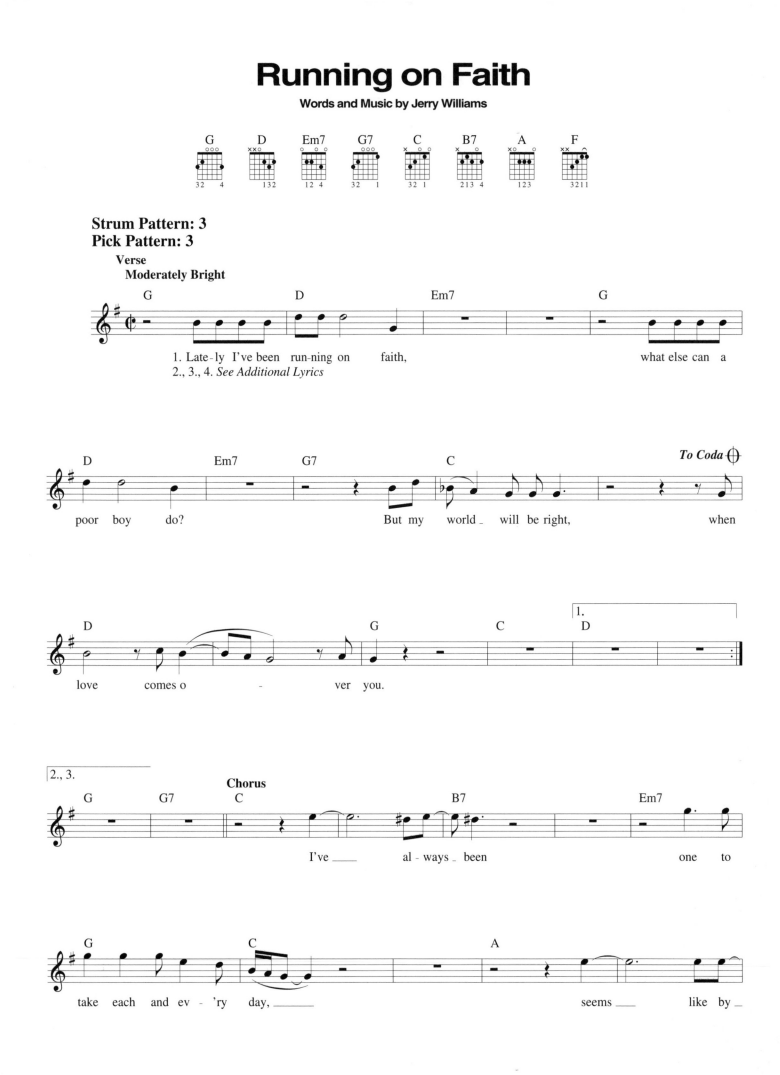

Running on Faith

Words and Music by Jerry Williams

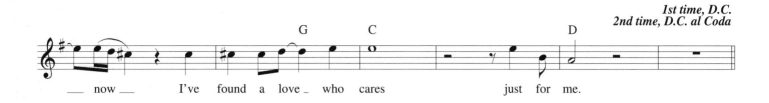

G   C   D

___ now ___   I've   found   a   love _   who   cares   just   for   me.

✛ *Coda*

D   F   C

love   comes   o   -   ver   you. ___

Outro   *Repeat and Fade*

F   G   F   C

When   love   comes   o   -   ver   you. ___   When

Additional Lyrics

2. Lately I've been talking in my sleep,
    Can't imagine what I'd have to say.
    Except my world will be right,
    When love comes back your way.

3. Then we'd go running on faith,
    All of our dreams will come true.
    And our world will be right,
    When love comes over me and you.

4. Then we'd go running on faith,
    All of our dreams will come true.
    All the world will be right,
    When love comes over you.

San Francisco Bay Blues

Words and Music by Jesse Fuller

Additional Lyrics

4. Meanwhile, livin' in the city, just about to go insane.
   All I heard my baby, Lord, wishin' you would call my name.
   If I ever get back to stay, it's gonna be another brand new day,
   Walkin' with my baby down by the San Francisco Bay, hey, hey.
   Walkin' with my baby down by the San Francisco Bay.

The Shape You're In

Words and Music by Eric Clapton

Additional Lyrics

2. My little girl really loves that wine.
   Wine will do it to her almost ev'ry time.
   If it's red or white, if it's in between,
   She can drink more wine than I've ever seen.

3. I'm not tryin' to get heavy with you.
   I'll mind my own bus'ness if you want me to.
   But I love you, girl I don't love no-one else.
   I'm just tellin' you, baby, 'cause I've been there myself.

She's Waiting

Words and Music by Eric Clapton and Peter Robinson

Additional Lyrics

3. I see the hunger burning in your eyes.
   Any fool could see there's something wrong.
   You keep pretending not to care,
   Well, I will hear you sing a different song.

Roll It Over

Words and Music by Eric Clapton and Bobby Whitlock

Strum Pattern: 1
Pick Pattern: 2

Verse
Moderate Blues

1. Go down eas - y and let me take my time. ___
2. *See Additional Lyrics*

Go down eas - y and let me take my time. ___

Rock me slow ___ till I lose my mind. ___

1.

2.

You don't know how ___

much it means ___ to be here in your arms. ___

Outro

___ Roll it o - ver. Roll it o - ver.

* sung 1st time

Additional Lyrics

2. Roll it over, let's take it from behind.
Roll it over, let's take it from behind.
S'only love, God knows it ain't no crime.

Signe

By Eric Clapton

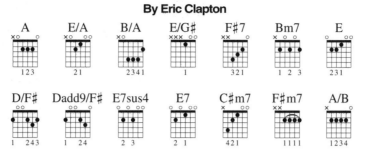

Strum Pattern: 6
Pick Pattern: 1

A Moderately Fast

Sleeping in the Ground

Words and Music by Sam Myers

Strum Pattern: 1
Pick Pattern: 2

Chorus
Moderate Shuffle

I would rath - er see you sleep - in' in the ground. ___

I would ___ rath - er see you ___ sleep - in' in ___ the

ground ___ than ___ to stay a - round here if you're gon - na put me down. ___

Verse

1. Well, I gave you all my mon - ey, ev - 'ry -

thing I o - own. Well, I gave you all my mon - ey, ev - 'ry - thing I

o - o - own. Well, some - day I'm gon - na get luck - y, ___

Someone Like You

Words and Music by Arthur Louis

Spoonful

Words and Music by Willie Dixon

Strum Pattern: 1
Pick Pattern: 2

1. Could fill a spoon's full of dia-monds, could fill a spoon's full of gold.
2., 3. *See Additional Lyrics*

Just a lit-tle spoon of your pre-cious love

sat - is - fy my soul. Men lies a - bout it;

some of them cries a - bout it. Some of them

dies a - bout it. Ev - 'ry-thing's a-fight-in' a - bout the

spoon - ful. That spoon, that spoon, that spoon - ful. That spoon, that spoon, that

spoon - ful. That spoon, that spoon, that spoon - ful. That spoon, that spoon, that

Additional Lyrics

2. Could fill a spoon's full of coffee;
Could fill a spoon's full of tea.
Just a little spoon of your precious love,
Is that enough for me?

3. Could fill a spoon's full of water,
Saved them from the desert sands.
Was a little spoon of your love, baby,
Saved you from another man.

Strange Brew

Words and Music by Eric Clapton, Felix Pappalardi and Gail Collins

Strum Pattern: 1
Pick Pattern: 2

Additional Lyrics

2. She's some kind of demon messin' in the glue.
   If you don't watch out, it'll stick to you.
   What kind of fool are you?
   Strange brew, killin' what's inside of you.

3. On a boat in the middle of the raging sea,
   She would make a scene for it all to be ignored,
   And wouldn't you be bored.
   Strange brew, killin' what's inside of you.

Sunshine of Your Love

Words and Music by Jack Bruce, Pete Brown and Eric Clapton

Additional Lyrics

2., 3. I'm with you my love,
The light shining through on you.
Yes, I'm with you my love.
It's the morning and just we two.
I'll stay with you, darling now.
I'll stay with you till my seeds are dried up.

Too Bad

Words and Music by Eric Clapton

Strum Pattern: 1
Pick Pattern: 2

Additional Lyrics

2. It's too bad I don't need you,
   'Cause we get along so good.
   It's too bad I don't need you,
   Because we get along so good.
   You must be thinking 'bout this time,
   That my poor heart is made of wood.

3. It's too bad I don't miss you,
   'Cause you're always on my mind.
   It's too bad I don't miss you,
   'Cause you're always on my mind.
   I want to stay around, li'l' silly girl,
   And learn to love you all the time.

Tales of Brave Ulysses

Words and Music by Eric Clapton and Martin Sharp

Strum Pattern: 3
Pick Pattern: 3

Additional Lyrics

3. And you see a girl's brown body dancing through the turquoise,
   And her footprints make you follow where the sky loves the sea;
   And when your fingers find her she drowns you in her body,
   Carving deep blue ripples in the tissues of your mind.

4. Tiny purple fishes run laughing through your fingers,
   And you want to take her with you to the hard land of the winter.

Tears in Heaven

featured in the Motion Picture RUSH

Words and Music by Eric Clapton and Will Jennings

Additional Lyrics

2. Would you hold my hand if I saw you in heaven?
   Would you help me stand if I saw you in heaven?

Chorus 2. I'll find my way through night and day,
   'Cause I know I just can't stay here in heaven.

Tell the Truth

Words and Music by Eric Clapton and Bobby Whitlock

Strum Pattern: 1
Pick Pattern: 2

Additional Lyrics

2. It doesn't matter who you are,
   Or where you're goin' or been.
   Open your eyes and look into your heart;

3. Hear what I say 'cause ev'ry word is true.
   You know I wouldn't tell you no lies.
   Your time's comin'. Gonna be soon, boy;

Thorn Tree in the Garden

Words and Music by Bobby Whitlock

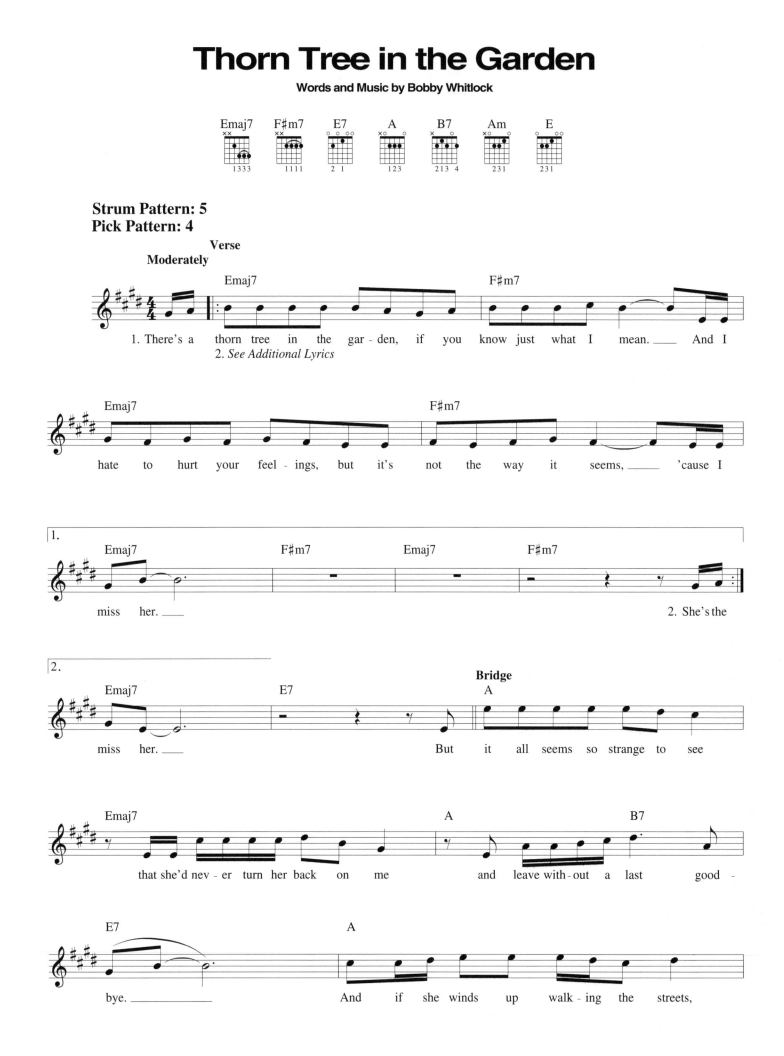

Strum Pattern: 5
Pick Pattern: 4

Verse
Moderately

1. There's a thorn tree in the gar-den, if you know just what I mean. And I
2. *See Additional Lyrics*

hate to hurt your feel-ings, but it's not the way it seems, 'cause I

1.
miss her. 2. She's the

2.
miss her.

Bridge

But it all seems so strange to see

that she'd nev-er turn her back on me and leave with-out a last good-

bye. And if she winds up walk-ing the streets,

Emaj7 ... A

lov - ing ev - 'ry oth - er man she meets, who'll be the one to an - swer

B7 ... Emaj7 ... E7

why?_____ Lord, I hope it's not me.

A ... Am ... E ... **Verse** Emaj7

3. And if I nev - er see her face a - gain, I

F#m7 ... Emaj7

nev - er hold her hand, and if she's in some - bod - y's arms, I

F#m7 ... Emaj7 ... E7

know I'll un - der - stand. _____ But I miss that girl. I

A ... Am ... **Outro** Emaj7 ... E7 ... A ... *Repeat and Fade* Am

still __ miss that girl.

Additional Lyrics

2. She's the only girl I've cared for, the only one I've known.
And no one ever shared more love than we've known.
And I miss her.

Tulsa Time

Words and Music by Danny Flowers

Strum Pattern: 1
Pick Pattern: 1

Verse
Moderate Boogie

1. I left O- kla- ho- ma driv- in' in a Pon- ti- ac,
2. *See Additional Lyrics*

just a- bout to lose __ my mind. __ I was goin' to Ar- i- zo- na, may- be

on to Cal- i- for- nia where the peo- ple all live __ so fine. __ My

ba- by said I's cra- zy. My mom- ma called me la- zy. I was goin' to show 'em all __ this time. __

'Cause you know I ain't no fool, 'n I don't need no more school- in'. I was

born to just walk __ the line. 1., 3. Liv- in' on Tul- sa time.
2. *See Additional Lyrics*

Chorus

Liv- in' on Tul- sa time. __ Well, you know I been through it when I

1.
set my watch back to it. Liv- in' on Tul- sa time. __

2. *D.S and Fade*
2. Well,

Additional Lyrics

2. Well, there I was in Hollywood,
Wishin' I was doing good,
Talkin' on the telephone line.
But they don't need me in the movies
And nobody sings my songs,
Guess I'm just a wastin' time.
Well, then I got to thinkin',
Man, I'm really sinkin'
And I really had a flash this time.
I had no bus'ness leavin' and nobody would be grievin'
If I went on back to Tulsa time.

Chorus 2 Livin' on Tulsa time.
Livin' on Tulsa time.
Gonna set my watch back to it,
'Cause you know I've been through it,
Livin' on Tulsa time.

Walkin' Blues

Words and Music by Robert Johnson

Strum Pattern: 1
Pick Pattern: 2

Verse
Moderate Slow Blues

1. Woke up this morn - in', feel 'round for my shoes. You know a-bout that, babe,
2., 3. *See Additional Lyrics*

I have that old walk-in' blues. Woke up this morn - in', I feel 'round for my

shoes. You know 'bout that ba - by, whoa,

Lord, I had them old walk - in' blues.

Additional Lyrics

2. I'm leavin' this mornin' I have to go ride the blinds.
   I been mistreated. I don't mind dyin'
   This a-mornin', if I have to go rob ya blind.
   I been mistreated, whoa, Lord, I don't mind dyin'.

3. People tell me the walkin' blues ain't bad,
   The worse old feelin' I most ever had.
   People tell me the old walkin' blues ain't bad.
   Well, it's the worse old feelin', whoa, Lord, the most I ever had.

Watch Out for Lucy

Words and Music by Eric Clapton

1. Now my friend Bill ___ was just a work - ing lad, ___ and he

2., 3. *See Additional Lyrics*

liked to have ___ his fun. ___ He'd like to find a girl ___ and get com -

- fort - 'ble ___ when his work - ing day ___ was done. ___

___ He would spend ___ all his mon - ey on a

Fri - day night, _ wake up in the morn - ing broke. ___ Well, he had ___

___ a run - in' ___ with lit - tle Lu - cy then, ___ be -

Chorus

lieve me that ain't no joke. ___ Watch out ___ for Lu -

- cy, though she may look frail. ___ Say ex - cuse ___

Additional Lyrics

2. She started out working in a cafe
   Picking money upon the side.
   She was free and easy, ev'rybody's friend,
   But she couldn't be satisfied.
   So now in walks Bill
   With cash in his hand,
   His heart upon his sleeve,
   We tried to warn him about her ways,
   We never did succeed.

3. Well, the trap was sprung for poor old Bill,
   You should have heard little Lucy sing:
   "I want a Cadillac car, a beautiful home,
   And a thousand dollar ring."
   They found our hero in the gutter
   With a diamond ring and a gun,
   He'd done it for the love of Lucy
   And ended up on the run.

Whatcha Gonna Do

Words and Music by Peter Tosh

Additional Lyrics

2. Next week, next week is the case
   'I'm 'ave a draped judge to face.
   'I'm 'ave the island sea in space
   Or make the doctor man work on his face.

3. Next door neighbor, them 'old your son.
   They say they find him with one gun.
   And there's no need to mention,
   I'm going to get an indefinite detention.

White Room

Words and Music by Jack Bruce and Pete Brown

Strum Pattern: 3
Pick Pattern: 3

Intro
Moderately

* let chords ring at 5/4 sections

1. In a

% Verse

white room   with black cur-tains   near the sta - tion.   Black roof coun - try,   no gold

2., 3. *See Additional Lyrics*

pave-ments,   tired _ star - lings.   Sil - ver hor - ses   ran down moon-beams   in your

dark eyes.   Dawn-light smiles   on you leav-ing   my con - tent - ment.

Chorus

1. I'll wait   in this place where the sun nev - er shines;   wait   in this

2., 3. *See Additional Lyrics*

Additional Lyrics

2. You said no strings could secure you at the station.
   Platform ticket, restless diesels, goodbye windows.
   I walked into such a sad time at the station.
   As I walked out, felt my own need just beginning.

Chorus 2. I'll wait in the queue when the trains come back,
   Lie with you where the shadows run from themselves.

3. At the party, she was kindness in the hard crowd.
   Consolation for the old wound now forgotten.
   Yellow tigers crouched in jungles in the dark eyes.
   She's just dressing, goodbye windows, tired starlings.

Chorus 3. I'll sleep in this place with the lonely crowd.
   Lie in the dark where the shadows run from themselves.

Wonderful Tonight

Words and Music by Eric Clapton

Strum Pattern: 4
Pick Pattern: 1

Intro
Moderately

1. It's late in the eve - ning; she's won-d'ring what clothes ___
2., 3. *See Additional Lyrics*

___ to wear. ___ She puts on her make - up and brush-es her long ___

___ blonde hair. ___ And then she asks ___ me, "Do I look all right?" ___

To Coda ⊕

___ And I say, "Yes, you look won - der - ful ___ to - night." ___

1.

Additional Lyrics

2. We go to a party, and ev'ryone turns to see.
   This beautiful lady is walking around with me.
   And then she asks me, "Do you feel alright?"
   And I say, "Yes, I feel wonderful tonight."

3. It's time to go home now, and I've got an aching head.
   So I give her the car keys, and she helps me to bed.
   And then I tell her, as I turn out the light,
   I say, "My darling, you are wonderful tonight."
   Oh, my darling, you are wonderful tonight.

Wrapping Paper

Words and Music by Jack Bruce and Peter Brown

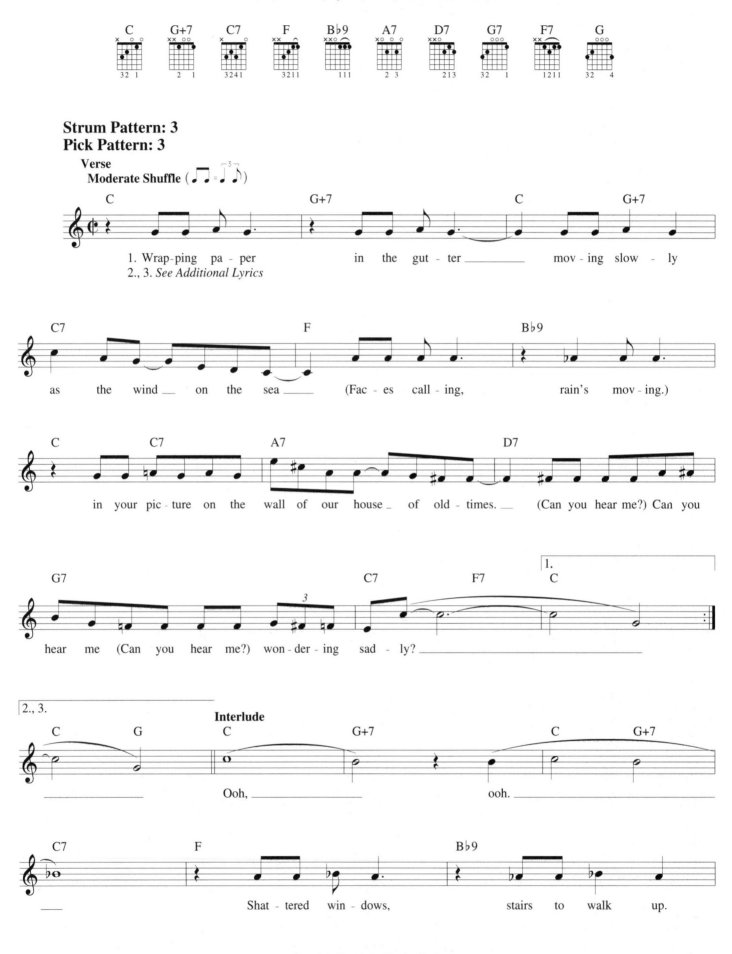

Strum Pattern: 3
Pick Pattern: 3

Verse
Moderate Shuffle

1. Wrap-ping pa-per   in the gut-ter ___ mov-ing slow-ly
2., 3. *See Additional Lyrics*

as the wind ___ on the sea ___ (Fac-es call-ing, rain's mov-ing.)

in your pic-ture on the wall of our house ___ of old-times. ___ (Can you hear me?) Can you

hear me (Can you hear me?) won-der-ing sad-ly? ___

Interlude

Ooh, ___ ooh. ___

Shat-tered win-dows, stairs to walk up.

Bridge

D.C. and Fade

Additional Lyrics

2. In the city, feeling pretty
   Down and out and making love to you on the shore.
   (Moving buildings, faces empty.)
   In the picture as I gaze ahead
   And don't see
   (That they're calling.) That they're calling,
   (That they're calling.) wondering sadly.

3. Someday I'll get back, somehow I'll do it.
   I'll arrive there and you'll be there to meet me.
   (All together, tread the weeds down.)
   Kiss again in the picture on the wall
   (Where I loved you.) in the old house,
   (Where I loved you.) loved you so well.

Willie and the Hand Jive

Words and Music by Johnny Otis

Strum Pattern: 1
Pick Pattern: 2

Verse
Moderate Bo Diddley Beat

1. I know a cat named Way-Out Willie.
2., 3., 4. *See Additional Lyrics*

Got a cool little chick named Rock-in' Millie.

He can walk and stroll and Su-sie Q,

and do that cra-zy hand jive too.

Hand-

Chorus

jive. Hand - jive. Hand - jive. Do-in' that cra-zy hand-

To Coda ⊕

D.C. al Coda
(take repeat)

jive.

⊕ *Coda*

jive.

Outro
Repeat and Fade

Additional Lyrics

2. Ma-ma, Ma-ma look at Uncle Joe.
   He's doin' the hand jive with sister Flo.
   Grandma gave baby sister a dime.
   "Do that hand jive one more time."

3. Doctor and a lawyer and an Indian cheif,
   They all dig that crazy beat.
   Way-Out Willie gave them all a treat.
   When he did that hand jive with his feet.

4. Willie and Millie got married last fall.
   They got a little Willie junior and that ain't all.
   Well, the kid's got crazy and it's plain to see,
   Doin' the hand jive on TV.